M O D E R 8™

BALANCE FOR A BETTER LIFE

How to Control Your Drinking and Learn to Drink in Moderation

ELIZABETH MICHAEL

ISBN: 1456375415
ISBN-13: 978-1456375416

CONTENTS

INTRODUCTION

Does this sound familiar? It's three in the morning and you've just regained consciousness after passing out from a full day of drinking. You can't sleep now because the alcohol won't let you. How much did you drink anyway? You can take inventory of empty bottles later after you take something for your splitting headache. How did it happen? How did you let one drink turn into who knows how many? What do you remember? Did you drive? Did you get into an argument with someone? Who saw you? That's it—you're tired of feeling bad and shameful...you're going to quit drinking...at least for a while. Somehow you manage to nod off to sleep just in time for your alarm to go off. Thank God you took the aspirin. Your head doesn't hurt as badly, but your mind is in a fog, your stomach is queasy, and your hands are shaking. You've had enough!

But somewhere around four in the afternoon, while the queasiness and fog are mostly gone, there's that anxious, impatient feeling. Everything gets on your nerves. OK—just one drink—and then you'll *really* quit tomorrow. But then one drink turns into five...six...ten...and the cycle continues.

Maybe your friends were right—maybe you *are* an alcoholic...maybe you *are* weak and damaged.

Or maybe you just need the skills and tools to stop this out-of-control cycle and get control once and for all!

Do you think it's possible?

WHAT TO EXPECT FROM THIS BOOK

I'm not a psychologist or an addiction specialist—I'm only someone who has battled alcohol abuse and won. While I do hold degrees in biochemistry and biology that have enabled me to understand the *science* behind addiction, it is my *experience* with alcohol that has lead me to develop the MODER8 system, a dietary supplement and program to help others drink in moderation. In this book are the tools and skills that I have learned and cultivated to beat alcoholism and to drink moderately.

There are many books advocating methods for learning how to stop drinking or to drink moderately. The reasons we drink and the characteristics of our drinking problems are just as vast.

Some of us slipped into problem drinking after drinking socially at one time in our lives. Others—like me—may never have known what drinking socially was like; we were never able to be satisfied with just one drink.

Scott Miller and Insoo Berg, in *The Miracle Method* stated that no one method of treatment works for everyone.[1] But *some* method works for almost anyone if they are willing and motivated to make the necessary changes. Just as individual as a person's appearance, personality, and fingerprints, so, too, will be your recovery.

HOW TO USE THIS GUIDE

The last thing you need is a bunch of words and theory to muddle through while your brain is glazed over by a hangover-induced fog. You'll find exercises and strategies to make immediate changes and to design your plan of action.

This book is divided into eight parts, or strategies:

- **Strategy I** is designed to change the way you think about alcoholism and to give you some food for thought when creating your own plan.

- **Strategy II** will help you understand the role that brain chemistry plays in addiction and how you can make changes to your chemistry.

- **Strategy III** gives you the tools and exercises to get motivated to make the necessary changes that will result in controlling your alcohol consumption.

- **Strategy IV** will help you discover and develop alternative experiences and activities to take the place of drinking.

- **Strategy V** will help you plan how and when you will drink.

- **Strategy VI** provides exercises and tools to help you identify the reasons that you drink and to learn to react and respond to them in healthy, more productive ways.

- **Strategy VII** will help you identify ways to get the external, nonjudgmental support that you need to help you work through your program.

- **Strategy VIII** will give you tools to ensure that old habits don't return once you've made your changes and gained control of your drinking.

For best results, skim through each section to see which ones resonate the most with you. Begin working on those exercises first. At the beginning of each strategy or exercise, you will see a checklist, or "take-away" information. Even if you don't have the time or desire to thoroughly read that section, at least be familiar with the take-away information.

You will begin to experience small changes and progress immediately. It may take several months to a year to get completely where you want to be, but you will get there if you continue to use these tools.

STRATEGY 1:

CHANGE THE WAY YOU THINK ABOUT ALCOHOLISM

CHANGE THE WAY YOU THINK ABOUT ALCOHOLISM AND ABSTINENCE

If you are one of the 95 percent of people that have tried Alcoholics Anonymous and left, don't be discouraged. The truth is, abstaining completely from alcohol, just like crash dieting or trying to abstain from anything that you regard as pleasurable, can be a recipe for failure.

Why? Because we often associate drinking, eating, and smoking with escaping from pain, and trying to completely remove those things sets us up for *more* discomfort. We feel deprived, punished, and eventually rebellious. We go back to our comfortable substance of choice with a vengeance, and in return we feel even worse about ourselves and our ability to control our bad habits. The negativity begins a spiral of out-of-control indulgence.

The answer is in changing your lifestyle and striving for balance and moderation.

AN AWAKENING

From this moment on, I want to change the way you think about drinking and challenge the myths you may have believed for years, which may have actually kept you trapped, believing you had a permanent problem that couldn't be overcome. I hope you will experience an awakening about the realities of alcohol addiction and gain awareness that you really do have the ability to take control.

MYTH

Alcoholism is a progressive *disease* and once someone drinks uncontrollably, they can never again drink socially.

FACT

The physical tolerance and, ultimately, physical and emotional addiction progresses over time, but it *is reversible. Habits can be changed.* Physical dependence can be eliminated; it just takes the willingness, self-awareness, tools, and effort.[2,3]

MYTH

Alcohol addiction is genetic. Because my grandparents were drunks and my parents were drunks, I am doomed. My only hope is complete abstinence.

FACT

While genetics does dictate metabolism and personality to a certain extent, what we have inherited from our parents and family is more *learned* behavior, including abusing alcohol and how we handle our emotions.[3]

YOU DO HAVE THE ABILITY TO CONTROL YOURSELF

So what we must begin to do is change the way we think about drinking! The concept isn't new. William James, a famous psychologist from the 1800s, said, "The greatest discovery of my generation is that human beings, by changing the inner attitudes of their minds, can change the outer aspects of their lives."[4] Essentially, if you believe you have no control over something—in this case, drinking—then you won't have control. Just think about what a great cop-out that can be: "It's genetic. I have no ability to control how much I drink. My father was an alcoholic, my grandfather was an alcoholic, and so I'm an alcoholic. I *have to drink* this twelve-pack of beer!"

Don't misunderstand me. I do believe that a genetic link to our personalities and our brain biochemistry may be a contributing factor in alcoholism. But I don't think we can use our genetics as an excuse.

BEWARE OF THE POWER OF NEGATIVE SUGGESTION

Be cautious about who and what you listen to. We as human beings can be quite vulnerable to suggestion. Here is an example of the power of a negative suggestion. "Janet" had been working on her program and drinking in moderation for about two years when a twenty-five-year veteran of Alcoholics Anonymous and addiction expert told Janet that it was impossible to drink in moderation if someone had ever had a drinking problem (and was therefore an alcoholic). According to the expert, the only real answer was complete abstinence. For a couple of weeks following that encounter, Janet was depressed and began to drink more than her routine limit. Janet called me one day to tell me her story, and I reminded her that the only thing that had changed was her mind! She had previously been successfully drinking moderately for almost two years! She's back on track with her program now.

FOCUS ON THE SOLUTION
Rather than thinking how bad you feel about yourself and then drinking, think about the version of you that you want to be without a drinking problem. What you focus on is what expands, so if you focus on how bad your drinking problem has become, guess what will get worse— your drinking!

The first step in developing a personal plan is determining why it's important to *you* to control your drinking. I put the emphasis on *you* because your own motivation is the only truly effective force. You can decide to quit because you got a DUI, or because your spouse has been complaining about "your problem," but those aren't true motivators. They ultimately make you feel trapped, helpless, or resentful. Over time, change due to external negative motivators is only temporary. Take some time to develop new goals and to rekindle old dreams. A positive reason to cut back on your drinking is so much more motivating than trying to slow down because you feel bad or guilty. You'll have a chance to work on this in the "Getting Motivated" section. Then you can focus on making those goals happen. You naturally will want to drink less, because drinking will get in the way of accomplishing those goals, and accomplishing those goals is a pleasant feeling. Visualize who you want to be and focus on being that person, versus focusing on the "drinking problem."

LIGHTEN UP!
We drink to get happy, get away from the serious and negative issues, or even to get away from our critical self-talk. So go ahead and lighten up without alcohol! Start having some alcohol-free fun and stop beating yourself up about your past. You may as well just go ahead and face the facts. We do stupid things when we're wasted! So what? Get over it and start living your life the way you want to, *now.*

ULTIMATELY, IT'S ABOUT CHOICES

If you learn nothing else from this book, begin asking yourself every time you start to drink, "Why do I want to drink and what are the consequences?"

For a long time, I drank because it helped me in uncomfortable social settings, but you know what's worse than feeling like you don't fit in? Making a fool of yourself! When I drank, I thought I was as tough as Trinity from the Matrix, as sexy as Jennifer Lopez, or as talented of a dancer as the Solid Gold Dancers (I guess I'm showing my age now). While this may sound a little comical, the truth is, I used alcohol to deal with a lot of situations that I just couldn't face sober. But as long as we keep using alcohol to handle the situations, the circumstances will never change, because we don't have the skills to handle them effectively without alcohol, and we won't develop the skills if we keep drinking to deal with them. At some point, we have to quit using alcohol to delay the inevitable and go ahead and deal with the things we're running from.

Every day, hour, and moment, we have decisions to make that steer the course of our life. We choose to get out of bed or not, to eat a nutritious or unhealthy breakfast or no breakfast at all, to go to work or do the laundry. Every decision we make affects our life.

The same goes for addictions and drinking. We can eat that box of doughnuts and undermine our fitness program, or not eat it and stay on our goal of being fit and thin. We can buy a hundred dollars' worth of lottery tickets and risk losing the money, or not buy the tickets and use the money for food, saving for a car, or other needs. We choose to take the first drink, then to take the next one. We choose to get behind the wheel of a car and drive after we've had too much to drink. And so it is our decisions that are responsible for the potential consequences—feeling like crap the next day, getting a DUI, or worse, potentially killing yourself or someone else.

I'm sure this isn't the first time you've heard this. In fact, it's a widely touted philosophy. However, **at some point it will resonate in *your***

core as the absolute foundation driving your journey toward controlled drinking.

If you're among those who've bought into the notion that you are unique, in that the soul of an addict is different, and you have a disease that prevents you from drinking any alcohol in a controlled fashion, then you *don't* have a choice. Your only option for living a healthy and productive life is to abstain from alcohol because according to this school of thought, "you are powerless."

However, for those of you who feel deep in your gut that this philosophy doesn't apply to you, let me give you some food for thought—and some tools for making better choices.

By nature, I believe humans tend to choose the most pleasant or rewarding choice for what is going on in their lives at the moment. Immediate gratification drives too many of us, however, so we need to develop the tools and to practice the techniques that will begin to steer our recovery; or perhaps a better way to put it is, "our ability to control substances."

In Strategies II–VIII discussed in this book, you'll begin to shift the balance of your life and out-of-control drinking by the daily choices you make. The choices you make should be based on the following:

- **Personal goals and values.** What is your life like right now? Are you content with your situation or do you feel trapped? In "Strategy III: Getting Motivated," you'll have the opportunity to create personal goals and to discover your dreams and passions. Having a positive reason not to drink will help drive your decisions. For example, if you've decided you're going to begin training for a triathlon, you aren't as likely to drink, or you'll drink less when you know the next morning you want to feel energetic and perform at your best so you can run six miles or swim a mile. Or, if you've decided to write and publish a book, you know you need to have your head clear so you can put coherent thoughts down on paper. I know a few of you are saying "Yeah, but I'm more creative when I'm drinking." Believe me, I understand how you feel. At some point, however, you need to get those words down on paper and pitch to a publisher and that requires a clear head. So if you're stuck in a situation where you're not motivated—a bad job or bad relationship—it's time to start making changes in your life toward meeting your goals.

- **Creating your drinking plan.** Creating a drinking plan ahead of time is important because you will have already done the thinking when you are in the right frame of mind. When you do start drinking, you can follow the plan without trying to make decisions while in an altered state. Know ahead of time what you'll do if you've drunk your planned amount and still want more. Know what your diversion will be and do it. The drive to have another drink will go away, and you will have gained the confidence of knowing that you *do* have the power to control your alcohol consumption. See "Strategy V: Developing a Drinking Plan" for more information.

- **If choosing abstinence, make the decision from a position of power, not from being powerless**. The truth is, abstinence is easier. Trying to learn to drink in moderation takes effort— remembering to take MODER8 or another dietary supplement, working on a program, and dealing with triggers and baggage all take work. But if you take into consideration that alcohol is a toxin, then it becomes even less attractive to keep alcohol in your life. If you've personally decided alcohol just doesn't fit into your life, then I commend you and admire your decision. Make sure you fill the void left by alcohol with healthy and positive activities and habits.

Ultimately, it's all about choices. If you get in the habit of thinking through your options and selecting choices that support your goals and values, your life will begin to take a different course and you'll find yourself in control, with greater confidence.

TAKE-AWAY CHECKLIST

1. Shift your brain chemistry in order to deal with stress, anxiety, and cravings.
2. Use brain-modulating dietary supplements.
3. Exercise and meditate to adjust the balance.
4. Use self-soothing techniques for peace and relaxation.

UNDERSTANDING BRAIN CHEMISTRY AND ADDICTION

Our emotions, craving, impulses, and ultimately our actions are dependent on a finely tuned system of brain chemicals called neurotransmitters. These neurotransmitters are either "positive or negative" and essentially either tell part of our brains to turn on or turn off. The balance of these neurotransmitters is critical for normal, healthy brain activity. But a deficiency or overproduction of any one of them can result in depression, anxiety, substance cravings, and even addictions.

Our genes program for the synthesis of the receptors and enzymes involved in utilizing and producing these neurotransmitters, which ultimately determines how well the neurotransmitters work. So while there is no "alcoholic gene," your genetics determines your innate brain chemistry and function that make it vulnerable to abusing a particular substance (food, drugs, alcohol) or a particular action (shopping, watching TV, gambling) that make you feel good or "balanced" by mimicking a deficient neurotransmitter.[5]

There are many neurotransmitters and hormones that play a role in determining how our brain functions and our behavior. The primary "negative," or inhibitory, neurotransmitters are gamma-aminobutyric acid or GABA, serotonin, and endorphins. GABA is associated with relaxation—mental more than emotional. Serotonin is more of an emotional relaxant. Endorphins are your body's natural painkiller and pleasure producer.

The primary "positive," or excitatory, neurotransmitters include dopamine, norepinephrine (sometimes called noradrenaline), and epinephrine (also known as adrenaline). Dopamine is the excitatory neurotransmitter responsible for pleasure, euphoria, and short-term intense concentration. Norepenephrine is responsible for sustained alertness. Norepenephrine and epinephrine are both associated with the "fight-or-flight" response in the body.

The excess firing of excitatory neurons can result in anxiety, panic attacks, obsessiveness, and other disorders. It is the job of the negative neurotransmitters, including GABA and serotonin, to turn off the excess firing and the effects of the excitatory neurons.

Dopamine, for example, while important for producing a feeling of well-being, the excess release can cause out-of-control behavior, such as binge drinking. GABA keeps the release of dopamine in check.[6]

So maintaining a critical balance and modulating the levels of each of these neurotransmitters are crucial for controlling cravings and addiction. There are many dietary supplements on the market, including MODER8 that can aid in regulating your neurotransmitter levels.

In addition to taking dietary supplements—or even pharmaceutical medications—to adjust your brain chemistry, there are other things you can do to help your own body adjust its neurotransmitter levels:

1. Become aware of what naturally gives you pleasure. Increase your serotonin and endorphins with activities such as:
   a. Meditation
   b. Exercise
   c. Sunlight/being outside
   d. Massage
   e. Laughter/comedy

2. Reduce things that cause overproduction of positive neurotransmitters. Be aware of substances and activities that cause you to feel anxious:
   a. Reduce amount of caffeine.
   b. Be aware of medications such as decongestants (like pseudoephedrine) that act like a stimulant.
   c. When possible, eliminate exposure to unnecessarily stressful situations or people that may push buttons or cause you to feel agitated.

Think about the healthy things that you can do to adjust your brain chemistry naturally and start incorporating them into your life.

MODER8 AND OTHER DIETARY SUPPLEMENTS

MODER8 is a dietary supplement intended to aid in handling stress and cravings. In the book, *Change Your Brain, Change Your Body*, Daniel G. Amen offers an in-depth look at the brain and the roles of the neurotransmitters.[6] MODER8 was formulated based on a few of these neurotransmitters—the primary ingredient being GABA. GABA (gamma-aminobutyric acid) and GABA boosters function to turn off the excess firing of nerves, resulting in feeling more calm and in control.[7] MODER8 contains a fairly high level of GABA, 700 mg., in order to address the controversial blood-brain barrier (BBB) issue. At high enough levels, certain substances are able to leak through the BBB and do not require active transport. MODER8 also contains 5-HTP (a serotonin booster that produces the feelings of happiness), L-Theanine and Vitamin B6 to boost GABA levels, and Vitamin B1, which is valuable in preventing brain damage from alcohol. I also supplement my MODER8 intake occasionally with additional 5-HTP and L-Tyrosine. MODER8 helps me reduce feelings of stress and anxiety. I sometimes take MODER8 to feel more peaceful during the evening dinner crunch, and I've heard of many others who take it on their way home from work. Taking one or two MODER8 capsules before a *planned* drinking event can help you stick to your drinking plan and prevent a binge.

However, you don't have to use MODER8 to achieve these effects. You can see what combination of amino acids and/or herbal supplements work best for you.

EXERCISE

In addition to taking MODER8 and other brain-modulating dietary supplements, perhaps the best form of stress reduction is physical activity and/or exercise for several reasons—it helps burn excess anxious energy, helps you feel more self-confident and accomplished, and the ultimate—the release of endorphins, the hormones that produce the feeling of euphoria and well-being.

If you're like I was, drinking alcohol packed on the pounds. And with the extra weight comes a negative spiral—stop working out because it's not working, feel worse about yourself, and start doing more self-destructive things. That all-or-nothing beast pops up its nasty head again.

But let me ask you this: When you've been active in the past, either in a regular sport, activity, or workout, how did you feel? You probably feel more alive. You had a slight buzz from the endorphins and you felt better about yourself.

Now that you're getting control of your drinking, why not start putting exercise or physical activity back into your life? If you've never been much for exercise, why not give it a try as a part of this new chapter you're starting in your life? It doesn't have to be painful. For some people, working out sounds too much like "work." Instead, identify a physical activity you enjoy, like dancing or hiking in the woods or walking on the beach.

Here are a few tips for getting started:

Step 1: Identify something you enjoy doing for exercise. If you like running or hitting the weights, awesome. If not, you can *dance* up a sweat just as well!

Step 2: Create goals. Make your goal something simple, like lose five pounds in three months, increase my bench press weight by thirty pounds, or lose my muffin top by spring.

Step 3: Schedule regular exercise sessions. Make it easy enough to work into your schedule or it won't happen. For example, twenty to thirty minutes of walking or dancing three days a week is doable. Determine the best time of day for you.

Step 4: See exercise as a contribution to your overall mental and physical health. This isn't punishment; this is something to help you feel better physically and mentally and to add more joy and balance to your life. And, hopefully, you'll be doing this *without* drinking!

MEDITATION, PRAYER, HYPNOSIS, SPIRITUALITY

On the opposite end of the spectrum from physical exertion are meditation, hypnosis, and self-soothing techniques. These techniques, while being performed completely still, can actually help "center" you and *prevent* feelings of stress and anxiety.

Meditation and hypnosis, as well as activities such as listening to a babbling brook, watching a fire burn in the fireplace, or taking a relaxing stroll on the beach, all help to increase feelings of peace and well-being. These activities also give you the opportunity to calmly think through negative thoughts, a chance to daydream and think about your goals and passions, and to feel grateful for the positive things in your life. They provide you with the setting and mindset to get in touch with yourself and your spirituality (however you think of it). They increase self-esteem and self-confidence as well as mindfulness and becoming aware of what is going on with you at the moment— especially when you have the urge to drink. Find a meditation or self-hypnosis program you like, perhaps searching an online bookstore or health food store. I like *The Best Guide to Meditation*, by Victor N. Davich.[8]

SELF-SOOTHING TECHNIQUES

Self-soothing can be instant thought- and feeling-changing tools that I don't think can ever be overused. Think of using your five senses to enjoy life and pamper or treat yourself.

- Use your eyes to look at something pleasant, like a sunset, fireplace, or flowers.

- Use your ears to listen to melodic or peaceful music, or any music that makes you feel good. Listen to birds sing or a babbling water feature.

- Use your sense of taste to sip on something soothing or healthy, like herb tea or mineral water, savor a gourmet meal or some refreshing, chilled fruit.

- Use your sense of smell to enjoy a scented candle, which can also be a visual benefit watching the flame and meditating, or enjoy your favorite perfume or fresh flowers.

- Use your sense of touch. Get a massage or pedicure, see if you can get your husband or children to brush your hair, pet your dog or your cat, hug a pillow, or snuggle in a cozy blanket.

Getting in touch with nature is another great tool. The awe and energy from nature—watching birds and hearing them sing, smelling a pine forest or herb garden, feeling the smoothness of a well-worn pebble or the softness of a flower petal—almost always makes me feel good.

And don't forget to BREATHE. Learn to take deep, cleansing breaths. Fill your lungs with oxygen, taking slow, deep breaths in and exhaling slowly and completely, as well. It's amazing how therapeutic these techniques can be if you just take a few moments to stop and do them. Use these *healthy* alternatives for stress-reduction, and the bottle will become less and less attractive.

STRATEGY III:

GETTING MOTIVATED

GETTING MOTIVATED

TAKE-AWAY CHECKLIST
1. Create a new purpose for your life for which to strive.
2. Break free of feeling hopeless and trapped.
3. Use the worksheet to help create personal goals.
4. Discover or rediscover your dreams and passions.

WHERE ARE YOU ON THE PLEASURE/PAIN PENDULUM?
It seems like most behavior and decisions in life are based on the levels of pleasure (or reward) versus pain, and which one is more important to us at the moment. When I was in the middle of a drinking binge, I used to think, "Why can't life just be like this all the time—this mellow, euphoric, peaceful feeling of being in an alcohol-induced state?" But the answer would eventually come, because that "state" was very difficult to maintain and "one-too-many" turned into fights, arguments, paranoid thoughts, blackouts, embarrassment, shame...and so on.

Finding the motivation to quit a bad habit, including breaking free from an alcohol addiction, can be a matter of adjusting your position on the pleasure/pain pendulum. So, where are you right now? Are you swinging toward pleasure or pain?

STARTING POINT—**PAIN**—The pain of anxiety, stress, shyness, anger, loneliness, etc., drives the urge to drink to relieve the pain.

SWING TO (UNHEALTHY) **PLEASURE**—The pendulum swings to "pleasure" as the alcohol produces euphoria, relaxation, numbness, and a false sense of happiness.

SWING TO **PAIN**—The pendulum swings back to greater "pain" because of feelings of shame, embarrassment from what we may have done or said while we were intoxicated, health problems, relationship problems, etc.

SWING TO (HEALTHY) **PLEASURE**—As the pain from drinking gets too bad and we try to stop drinking on our own, we begin to feel more energetic, more productive, confident, hopeful, and in control.

THIS IS WHERE WE NEED TO STAY! But this is a very crucial time, because some of the original pain will still be there (anxiety, stress, anger, etc.) although we may have forgotten about the greater pain from abusing alcohol that led us to cut back on our drinking. This leaves us vulnerable to turning to alcohol again to address the painful emotions. We have two choices:

1) Start the pendulum swinging again by drinking to achieve the unhealthy pleasure—euphoria, numbness, relaxation, *or...*

2) Begin to put more energy into maintaining the "Healthy Pleasure" side of the pendulum by:
   a. Addressing the triggers that are causing you to feel pain.
   b. Find more healthy sources of pleasure, and replace alcohol with these alternatives. See "Strategy IV: Things to Do Instead of Drink" for more information.
   c. Balance your brain chemistry with supplements such as MODER8, 5-HTP, or L-Theanine.
   d. Set some personal goals in the various areas of your life. See "Setting Life Goals."
   e. Incorporate regular exercise in your life—make it fun, such as hiking, dancing, or swimming.

The more effort you put toward the "Healthy Pleasure" position on the pendulum while you're there, the easier it will be to stay there!

FINDING YOUR TRUE MOTIVATORS

Health issues and relationship conflicts usually are not great enough motivators to make us stop or cut back on our drinking. Instead, you have to dig deeper...to find what really motivates you.

For example, "Donna," after years of hiding her heavy drinking from the outside world, and arguing with her husband to just leave her alone about her drinking, she finally reached a point where she was sick and tired of feeling sick and tired...and tired of feeling bad about what little she had accomplished in her life. At fifty-three years old, Donna felt that half of her life was over—and her most important accomplishment in life—raising three children—was a blur of a memory. Donna was determined not to waste the rest of this life that she had been given by going through it in an alcohol-induced coma. Instead, she decided to start living life (with all of its pleasure and pain) sober. She was bound and determined that she would be around to experience her grandchildren with a healthy mind and body.

Ask yourself what is *your* true motivator...not what you think it should be or what the outside world will tell you it should be, but what is *your* innermost driving motivator?

SETTING NEW GOALS AND REKINDLING OLD DREAMS

I find that many people turn to abusing substances because they feel trapped or hopeless. They've reached a point in their lives or jobs or relationships where they feel, "It's all over, so why not just drink to tolerate it." I'm here to tell you that the old adage, "If you aren't growing, then you're dying," couldn't be more true than in the case of alcohol abuse and drinking in order to medicate the feelings of hopelessness.

For many adults—especially those of us over the age of thirty-five—setting goals and developing dreams stopped sometime after we graduated from college, got a job, or started a family. It's so easy to get caught in a rut, going through life taking care of the necessary tasks and chores, that we forget about setting and achieving personal goals or striving to realize new dreams. Without something to look forward to, it's easy to turn to alcohol as the only source of escape. Take some time and begin thinking about what you would want to do if you knew the world was about to end and money was no object. This should give you an idea of how to get started creating something to which you can look forward.

A *positive* reason to cut back on your drinking is so much more motivating than trying to slow down because you feel bad or guilty. You may have a spouse or friends urging you to quit drinking, placing labels on you like "alcoholic," or accusing you of not caring enough about them. This isn't motivational—in fact, it only produces shame and resentment, which ultimately will make you want to drink more to escape the negative feelings. Instead, do it for *you* because there is something or some purpose for which you want to *LIVE* instead of just waiting to *DIE.*

SETTING PERSONAL GOALS

Step 1: In your mind's image of your ideal world, your life would look like this in each category of your life. (Fill in the blanks.)

Self:

- Physical Health (physical strength, energy, stamina) _____

_____

_____

_____

- Appearance/Weight _____

_____

_____

_____

- Mental State (clarity, alertness, educational challenge) _____

_____

_____

_____

- Emotional State (happiness, satisfaction, content, self-confidence)

_____

_____

_____

- Spirituality (as you define it) _____

_____

_____

_____

Family:_____

_____

_____

Environment (home, location): _____

_____

_____

_____

Work/Volunteer Work: _____

_____

_____

Money: _____

_____

_____

_____

Hobbies/Leisure: _____

_____

_____

Step 2: Now determine how close you are to "ideal" in each of these areas on a scale of 0 to10 (0 being furthest from and 10 being closest to ideal).

Self:

- Physical/Health ___

- Physical/Appearance ___

- Mental State___

- Emotional State___

- Spirituality ___

Family: ___

Environment: ___

Work/Volunteer Work: ___

Money: ___

Hobbies/Leisure: ___

Step 3: What are the hurdles keeping you from reaching a 10 in each area?

Self:

- Physical Health (physical strength, energy, stamina) _____
  _____
  _____
  _____

- Appearance/Weight _____
  _____
  _____
  _____

- Mental State (clarity, alertness, educational challenge) _____
  _____
  _____
  _____

- Emotional State (happiness, satisfaction, content, self-confidence)
  _____
  _____
  _____

- Spirituality (as you define it) _____
  _____
  _____
  _____

Family:_____
  _____
  _____

Environment (home, location): _____

_____

_____

_____

Work/Volunteer Work: _____

_____

_____

Money: _____

_____

_____

Hobbies/Leisure: _____

_____

_____

Step 4: What actions can you take to overcome the hurdles you listed for each area?

Self:

- Physical Health (physical strength, energy, stamina) _____

_____

_____

_____

- Appearance/Weight _____

_____

_____

_____

- Mental State (clarity, alertness, educational challenge) _____

_____

_____

_____

- Emotional State (happiness, satisfaction, content, self-confidence)

  _____

  _____

  _____

- Spirituality (as you define it) _____

  _____

  _____

  _____

Family: _____

_____

_____

Environment (home, location): _____

_____

_____

_____

Work/Volunteer Work: _____

_____

_____

Money: _____

_____

_____

Hobbies/Leisure: _____

_____

_____

Step 5: Rank the areas by most important or most desirable to least important to you (1 = most important/desirable.)

Self:

- Physical/Health ___

- Physical/Appearance ___

- Mental State___

- Emotional State___

- Spiritual State___

Family: ___

Environment: ___

Work/Volunteer Work: ___

Money: ___

Hobbies/Leisure: ___

Step 6: Now rank the areas by easiest to accomplish based on the hurdles you listed and the actions necessary to overcome (1 = easiest.)

Self:

- Physical/Health ___

- Physical/Appearance ___

- Mental State___

- Emotional State___

- Spiritual State___

Family: ___

Environment: ___

Work/Volunteer Work: ___

Money: ___

Hobbies/Leisure: ___

Step 7: Now select the #1 area from each list—the most important/ desirable and the easiest. *These are the two goals on which you should begin to focus.* One will obviously be short-term and easy to achieve and the other will probably be more long-term, but more rewarding. Once you've achieved these goals, begin to choose from the rest of your list.

REKINDLING DREAMS

Do you remember when you were a child and someone would ask, "What do you want to be when you grow up?" Do you remember what you said? Do you remember what you felt?

So many of us got bogged down by things that happened in life that we just sort of gave up or lost focus on accomplishing our dreams. Some things were out of our control, and some were because of our own self-defeating behaviors, like choosing to party. At some point, alcohol either took the place of or helped to quench the innate drive we had to dream and to accomplish those dreams.

Now is the time to get back in touch with, or even discover for the first time in your life, what your passions and dreams are. You know you have gifts and skills you aren't using. Many of you probably feel guilty knowing you have them but aren't using them. Don't leave this world with your dreams unfulfilled. Identify them and begin to realize them.

Of course, the first step is figuring out what they are if you've buried them deep in a fog of alcohol and everyday life routine. Allow yourself to relax and let your mind wander. Find a quiet place where you have some privacy and won't be disturbed. Close your eyes and take a few deep breaths. Now ask yourself, "What am I truly passionate about?" "What makes me happy inside when I think about it?" "What would I do if money were no object?"

Step 1: Start writing what you hear. _____

_____

_____

_____

Step 2: Now identify your top one or two things.

_____

_____

_____

_____

Step 3: Is there something in the way of you living or accomplishing your dreams or passions? If yes, then write down the main issues.

_____

_____

_____

_____

Step 4: Begin creating an action plan to overcome those hurdles. For example:

1. **Dream**: To move to South Florida and start a charter fishing service.

2. **Hurdle:** I live in Atlanta and my children don't want to leave their friends. Plus, I don't have the money or connections to relocate or start that type of a business.

3. **Action Plan:**
   - Research what it actually takes to run such a business. What type of boat? How much do they generally cost? What type of regulations are involved or licenses required?

   - My youngest child will be graduating from high school in five years. I'll just continue to do the homework, save money, and do what I need to until then.

- In five years, my wife and I will move to Florida and start our dream business.

This is a bit simplified, but it gives you an understanding of where to start taking action. You don't have to wait around, or even completely dismiss your dreams, because of your current set of circumstances. Have the courage to change the things you can.

Start now! Begin working out your plan on the next page. (Use your own paper if you need more space.)

MY DREAM PLAN

I am passionate about:

My most fulfilling dream is to:

What is keeping me from accomplishing my dream?

Following are the steps I'll take to accomplish my dream:

1. _____

2. _____

3. _____

4. _____

5. _____

Date I plan to have accomplished my dream: _____

VISUALIZATION AND CREATING YOUR MANTRA

Visualize daily the person you want to be, doing the things that you want to be doing—without any of the barriers or hurdles that you believe are preventing you from doing them. See yourself living the life that you want to be living—healthy, happy, and in control of alcohol.

The more you focus on who you want to be and where you want to be, the less you will have the desire to drink, because it will get in the way of accomplishing your goals and dreams!

CREATE YOUR MANTRA, OR MOTTO

Develop your own personal mantra that you say to yourself every time you think about drinking or if you've reached your predetermined limit of your drinking plan. Dr. Pamela Peeke, author of *Body for Life for Women*,[9] recommends this type of technique for weight loss and fitness goals. I've created a modification of her method:

> **Step 1**—Basically, determine the consequences of out-of-control drinking, controlled drinking, or even not drinking. For example, the consequences of drinking too much are a hangover, headache, foggy head, and shame. The consequences of controlled drinking are self-confidence, a clear head, and energy to accomplish goals, peace, and contentment.

> **Step 2**—Your mantra should include running from the bad consequences and running to the positive. You mantra would be: "*Run from* hangover, headache, foggy head: *Run to* self-confidence, a clear head, and energy to accomplish goals, peace, and contentment."

If this type of mantra doesn't work, try something else to which you can better relate. For instance, some ladies in our online support group visualize a version of the "Good Wolf/Evil Wolf" parable. The condensed version goes something like this:

"Inside each of us are two wolves fighting—one is evil and one is good. The Evil Wolf is anger, envy, sorrow, regret, greed, arrogance, self-pity, guilt, resentment, inferiority, lies, false pride, superiority, and ego.

The Good Wolf is joy, peace, love, hope, serenity, humility, kindness, benevolence, empathy, generosity, truth, compassion, and faith. How do we determine which wolf wins? The one we feed the most."

Our drinking habits and behaviors can be like this. The more we drink to deal with emotional baggage, triggers, and habits, the more we feed our "Evil Drinking Wolf." We feel worse about ourselves. Our depression and paranoid thoughts increase the more we drink. However, the more we fill our life with positive thoughts and activities, work through our triggers and emotions, take our MODER8 or brain-modulating supplements, and work toward our goals and dreams, the more we feed our "Good Drinking Wolf" and the more in control our drinking will be. An example of the mantra would be "*Feed the Positive—Starve the Negative.*"

Wolf Parable Image by Anonymous Artist

Perhaps you're more of a computer programmer or machine operator, in which case "crap in, crap out" may make more sense to you. Whatever works to help you make the best decision, then use it—*but use something*! **The important thing is to find something effective to keep in your head and to say to yourself that will help you make good decisions about drinking and using the tools and strategies.**

MOTIVATION RESUSCITATION

So where do you find the motivation when you're stuck in the self-destructive quicksand of drinking to take the edge off of the hangover from last night's binge, then hating yourself and feeling hopeless because you believe that you are incapable of controlling alcohol?

Change your activities or your environment. Jump-start your motivation like you would jump-start a dead battery on your car or use a defibrillator to get your heart pumping again. It's not gradual; it's a sudden spark of new energy—something that brings you joy and makes you feel better about yourself immediately!

1) **Make the decision to start new today!**

2) **Break out of isolation!** Usually we are isolated when we are in this sludge, so pick up the phone and call someone or email a friend and make a lunch date for one of your favorite restaurants.

3) **Walk outside and take a deep breath,** then start pulling weeds from your garden or water your flowers, or simply go for a walk.

4) **Start planning for the "witching hour."** You know what time that is...sometime around 3 or 4 p.m. when you begin to tell yourself that it's OK to have "just one drink." Trust me, when you're stuck in the quicksand, you won't have just one drink...it's time to break the cycle. Plan ahead of time what you are going to do that is relaxing, pleasurable, or entertaining (depending on what you need. See "Strategy IV: Things to Do Instead of Drink" to help with this exercise).

5) **Don't let your shame hold you hostage and keep you paralyzed!**

STRATEGY IV:

THINGS TO DO INSTEAD OF DRINK

THINGS TO DO INSTEAD OF DRINK

TAKE-AWAY CHECKLIST
1. Find healthy, positive alternatives to drinking.
2. Determine other forms of pleasure, entertainment, and relaxation.
3. Try to include as many of these in your life as possible.

To be very honest with you, I have yet to find something that makes me feel the way alcohol makes me feel—but it is a false sense of euphoria and well-being that can result in negative consequences.

Sometimes we get so caught up in our everyday routine that we lose touch with what we like to do for fun. Drinking has become our only source of pleasure or our reward for trudging through our daily responsibilities. We forget about the healthy things we used to do for entertainment or relaxation.

You do need to have some alternatives to drinking or else you will allow old habits to take over.

Step 1: Use the worksheet on the next page to help do a little self-discovery. Set aside thirty minutes to an hour and let your mind wander to the things you used to do for enjoyment. The worksheet has a few examples to get you started. It's divided into three separate columns— "Relaxing/Leisure," "Creative," and "Productive"—because sometimes we drink due to stress, sometimes we drink because we're bored, and sometimes we drink because we just don't know what else to do. See "Self-Soothing Techniques" under "Strategy II: Changing Your Brain Chemistry," for more ideas.)

In addition to any relaxing hobbies you may consider, volunteer or charity work may be something to consider as well in your "productive" category of alternatives to drinking. I realize that if you're one of those stressed-out, overworked breadwinners or full-time moms, you're saying, "Give me a break. If I take on one more thing, I'm going to explode." But volunteer work can be very therapeutic. It feels good to do something for someone else, and it helps take the focus off of you, your problems, and even drinking!

Step 2: Once you've made the list, go back and circle the top five things in each category. Keep the list in a convenient place and refer to it when you want to drink due to boredom. Keep in mind: You are getting control of your life again, so live it!

Pleasurable and Rewarding Activities to Do Instead of Drinking
(Positive Activities to Include in Your Day)

"Relaxing/Leisure" (Low Mental or Physical Energy Required)	"Creative" (Moderate Mental or Physical Energy Required)	"Productive" (Higher Mental or Physical Energy Required)
• Read	• Cook/Bake	• Plan a business
• Sit outdoors	• Create recipes	• Volunteer work
• Meditate	• Write a cookbook	• Exercise
• Stroll in park	• Paint a picture	• Work out
• Stretch	• Color	• Organize a closet
• Take a bath	• Plan what to do if you win the lottery	• Design and decorate a room
• Nap	• Practice new makeup techniques (see great tutorials on Youtube.com)	• Paint a room a new color
• Listen to self-hypnosis tapes	• Start a fish tank	• Plant a garden
•	•	•
•	•	•
•	•	•
•	•	•
•	•	•
•	•	•
•	•	•
•	•	•

Now circle your top five activities from each of the lists above. Keep them close so you can find them easily when you're thinking about drinking because you're bored or you need to do something fun, stimulating, or peaceful.

INCORPORATE EIGHT POSITIVE THINGS INTO YOUR LIFE EVERY DAY

Essentially, you need to incorporate more activities that produce positive feelings and emotions into your life. I recommend eight each day because it's a number that can be associated with MODER8 and therefore easily remembered. It is not required, but is something to strive for in order to shift your focus to treating yourself better and creating a happier life. The happier and more balanced we are, the less we feel the urge to drink.

STRATEGY V:

DEVELOPING A DRINKING PLAN

DEVELOPING A DRINKING PLAN

TAKE-AWAY CHECKLIST
1. Determine your goals and what your drinking plan will help you achieve.
2. Plan out your drink limit per day.
3. Strive for alcohol-free days.
4. Develop a safety plan for how to derail the binge.

Just like designing the perfect diet and exercise routine to meet your health goals, it's important to develop your drinking plan and routine—at least for the first year or so until you learn new habits, make some self-discoveries, and gain confidence that you have the ability to control the amount you drink.

Step 1: First, determine what your goals are and why.

- Is it for health or safety-risk reduction?

- Maybe you just want to cut your alcohol consumption in half for now.

Step 2: Then plan out your drink limit per day. For example, if your goal is to feel good and have a clear head the next day, make your limit two or three drinks.

Step 3: Strive for alcohol-free days for a few reasons:

- To reduce your tolerance and the amount of alcohol it takes to feel satisfied.

- To reduce physical and emotional dependence on alcohol.

- To clear your mind so you can process emotions more accurately and effectively.

Determine how you will incorporate MODER8 or other dietary supplements into your plan to achieve your drinking goals.

Step 4: Develop a safety plan for how to derail the binge.

How many times have you set out to drink just one drink and then found yourself hung-over and unaware of what you may have done during your binge the night before? You get that anxious feeling and hurry to the refrigerator for a quick inventory, checking to see the number of beers that are left so you'll know just how badly you blew it the night before.

Or maybe you're already moderating your drinking, and although you're much better at controlling it, you're still drinking more than you plan or want. Let me give you a few tricks that have worked for others and myself.

Put together a plan ahead of time for what you'll do when you get to your limit. For example, my limit is three drinks. If I get to three drinks and the monster inside starts asking for more, I either change activities—like stand up, go to another room, and start working on something else to distract me—or I change what I'm consuming to something equally stimulating but nonalcoholic.

Distractions:
- Start reading or doing something that requires concentration.

- Shop online (not recommended if you've already gone way past your limit of drinks!).

- Take a walk or start working in the yard or on a project.

- If you're at a party, start talking to someone about something you need to be able to think clearly about in order to contribute better to the conversation.

Switch Beverages or Food:
- Make it "desert time" and get a small bite of something very flavorful, along with a cup of decaf coffee or tea.

- Drink a glass of ice water or mineral water and quench your thirst! Have you ever noticed that the more alcohol you drink, the thirstier you get, and so the more alcohol you drink? That's because your body needs *water*!

- Are you hungry? Get a healthy snack and a nonalcoholic beverage.

Moderate drinking skills take practice. These are just a few tips, but the more you use them, the better you'll be at controlled drinking and the more self-confident you'll feel.

MY SUPPLEMENT AND DRINKING PLAN

1. Goal or Objective:

    _____

    _____

2. Take MODER8 or other dietary supplement _____ times per day:

    *   # of capsules in morning (0–2): _____

    *   # of capsules in afternoon (0–2): _____

3. Take MODER8 supplement thirty minutes to an hour before drinking:

    *   # of drinks I'll drink in a six-hour period: _____

    *   # of drinks I'll drink in one day: _____

    *   # of days in a row I will drink: _____

    *   # of days in a week I will drink: _____

4. My Plan to Derail a Binge:

    _____

    _____

    _____

STRATEGY VI:

TRIGGERS/HABITS/STIMULI

IDENTIFYING DRINKING TRIGGERS

TAKE-AWAY CHECKLIST
1. Identify your drinking triggers.
2. Determine whether or not you have ability to change the situation.
3. Make plan for how you will deal with the trigger next time it happens.

We all know alcoholism is a complex, multifaceted problem. While much of it is biological, a lot of it is behavioral and emotional. That means we have to learn how to stop abusing alcohol. While products like MODER8 and other dietary supplements help to address the physical issues, only *you* can change your behavior.

One of the first things to do is to determine what the usual drinking triggers are, then determine the healthy, alcohol-free way to deal with them. Members of many twelve-step programs, including AA, recite the Serenity Prayer at every meeting. It goes something like this: "God, grant me the serenity to accept the things I cannot change, courage to change the things I can, and the wisdom to know the difference."

Here's a hint. Changing behavior usually involves changing how *you* react, not changing someone or something else. You also should have a plan in place for how you are going to deal with these things now, before they arise again.

Step 1: Identify your buttons or "triggers"—the things that usually send you to the bottle. Start a log and begin noticing the things that initiate that "I've got to have a drink!" feeling, or use the worksheet on page 51.

Step 2: Determine whether or not there is anything you can do to change it. This can be the most difficult step—figuring out whether or not you have any control over the issue. There may be a situation that we're allowing to continue because we don't want to stir up conflict, so we continue drowning our feelings and emotions instead of taking action. On the other side of the coin, there may be a situation that we truly cannot change, in which case we have to *accept* the fact we cannot change it and determine how we can change the way we *react* to the issue.

Step 3: Plan (ahead of time) for how you will deal with the trigger. For example, if your children make you nuts because they're fighting all the time, find a good parenting book and use the tools they recommend for dealing with sibling rivalry. Count to ten or walk out of the room. Whatever you do, do not drink to deal with the issue. That is *not* a part of drinking in moderation; that is full-blown alcoholism at its best. It you're really thinking about having a drink, remember what the result will be if you chose to drink instead of dealing with these issues head-on.

BE READY FOR THE UNEXPECTED

In addition to planning for your known triggers, plan for the unknown as well. Life consists of ups and downs, so as perfect as we can try to make our lives, adversity will happen. The important thing is how we choose to deal with it.

We can all find (and *do* find) reasons and excuses to drink. Some reasons cause very real, valid pain, but drinking isn't a part of the solution. Drinking adds to the problem. Instead, begin to picture yourself as a warrior, if you will, ready to take on the challenges that are going to arise and cause you to want to drink. Know that unexpected things are going to happen, and be ready to take the desire to drink and turn it into strength to stay true to yourself and your commitment. At the moment that you think, "I've just got to have a drink to deal with this," or even, "I deserve to drink because of this," make it your routine to turn to your own personal toolbox of alternate ways to cope.

THINKING THROUGH THE DRINK

Before you pour that first drink, *think through the drink*. How many drinks are you going to drink? Have you taken MODER8 or another brain-modulating dietary supplement first? If you drink just one, what are you going to do afterward? If you're going to drink two drinks, how fast do you plan to drink them? Let's say you've slammed two drinks down in about an hour and now you're thinking about a third. You have a choice. You can drink another and feel foggy and shaky the next morning—preventing you from performing as well at your responsibilities—or you can stop at two drinks. You can get up from where you are and change the direction of your focus. Go make a pot of decaf coffee, switch to drinking water, get online and shop, read a book, or take a walk. The next day, you'll wake up clear-headed and motivated to hit the ground running toward your goals.

KNOW *WHY* YOU'RE DRINKING BEFORE YOU TAKE THE FIRST SIP

If you are drinking because you're angry, lonely, bored, tired, hungry, thirsty, depressed, or any reason other than because you'd like to sip on a nice wine or a flavorful cocktail, then don't drink! If you are drinking to escape your feelings, it's more difficult to control the amount you drink and can lead to drinking more than you planned. You'll get a chance to work on this in more in "Learning to Control Your Emotions," "Removing Stimuli/Changing Habits," and "Get Out of the Rut and Dump the Baggage."

Plan for Dealing with Drinking Triggers

Identified "Button" or Trigger	Is there anything I can do about it?	How do *I* deal with it?
Example: "I like to drink wine or a cold beer while I cook."	**Example:** Definitely	**Example:** Instead of drinking an alcoholic beverage, I can sip on something else that I find pleasurable. In summer, I like an icy cold diet soda or even water! In the winter, I like to sip on a cup of coffee or hot herb tea.
Example: "It kills me that my children have to go stay with my jerk of an ex-husband every other weekend!"	**Example:** Unfortunately, not really.	**Example:** I have to keep my mind busy on things I enjoy, like spending time with my new husband, reading a really good book, working on home improvement projects or doing the things I can't really do when the children are home, like going to an expensive, fancy restaurant or R-rated movie.

LEARNING TO CONTROL YOUR EMOTIONS

TAKE-AWAY CHECKLIST
1. Gain short-term control over emotions by self-soothing and distracting instead of drinking.
2. Get long-term control over emotions by:
   a. Relaxing and trying to focus on the situation.
   b. Asking, "What am I feeling?"
   c. Getting logical.
   d. Getting wise.

I'm going to preface this section by saying that I could—and probably should—do an entire book on this subject alone, because when all the habits have been changed and the drinking plans are in place, dietary supplements are taken regularly, and so on, how we deal with emotions, especially pain or anxiety, will dictate how successful we are at controlling our drinking and ultimately how happy we are.

LEARNING TO CONTROL YOUR EMOTIONS IN THE SHORT-TERM
- Distract yourself by moving your focus to something else, like reading a book, calling a friend, or working out.

- Do one of the self-soothing activities from "Strategy II: Changing Your Brain Chemistry," such as taking a bath, lighting a candle, or going for a nature walk.

LEARNING TO CONTROL YOUR EMOTIONS IN THE LONG-TERM

Step 1: Breathe and then get in touch with the situation and your emotion.

Step 2: Ask yourself what emotion you're feeling—anger, sadness, jealousy, fear—and determine what you're telling yourself while you're in this emotional state. It is easy to blow things out of proportion and make things more catastrophic than they are. For example, "I'm feeling fearful because my husband just lost his job, and I'm afraid we'll lose this house that I love and become homeless."

Step 3: Then, get logical. Like a reporter, simply state the facts. For instance:

- My husband lost his job two days ago.

- We have enough money in the bank to cover two months of bills.

- My husband has a resume, but it needs to be updated.

- I don't currently have a job, and I'd prefer not to have to work right now because I need to be here for the kids.

Step 4: Once you're being logical and not emotional, get wise:

- We have time for my husband to find employment before we're late on our bills.

- I could get a part-time job to help out for a while, and my mom can be here for the kids.

- It's not productive for me to be fearful because it only causes me to do self-destructive things, like drink too much and worry excessively.

- Instead of drinking, I can start looking in the classifieds to see if there's anything I may be interested in doing part-time.

- I can self-soothe by taking a bath, working out, or distracting myself by calling a friend.

This is an example of how you can begin gaining control of your emotions. It takes practice, but this is a very important skill that, once you begin to master, can change your life in a very positive way. For a deeper look at emotion-controlling skills, you may want to find some books on cognitive behavioral therapy or dialectical behavior therapy.

REMOVING STIMULI/CHANGING HABITS

TAKE-AWAY CHECKLIST
1. Determine which stimuli produce the conditioned response to drink.
2. Develop alcohol-free alternatives to drinking.
3. Plan how to deal with the stimuli.

We're all familiar with Pavlov's dog and the "conditioned response." Basically, Pavlov would ring a bell (or some other type of signal) when he fed his dogs. Initially the dogs would salivate because they were being fed. But eventually Pavlov could simply ring the bell and the dogs would begin to salivate. I believe some of our drinking habits and cravings are like this. The habit also gets tied into the reward system. For instance, if we're used to drinking a glass of wine when we cook dinner or we swing by the pub when we leave work, then we eventually begin to associate cooking dinner or leaving work with drinking.

So what do you do?

- **In the beginning, find a different, but equally pleasant or rewarding, activity to take the place of drinking during those usual times of craving.** I recommend replacing the alcoholic drink with something nonalcoholic but tasty. Whenever I feel the urge to drink during one of those "habit" times, I usually take MODER8 because it cuts the stress and helps me feel more relaxed. Then I'll pour a cup of decaffeinated coffee or diet drink. I've heard of other creative "mocktails" that incorporate sparkling waters with juices; it's up to you as to how inventive you'd like to get. You can go online for a few other ideas: http://cocktails.about.com/od/mocktailmocktail/Mocktail_Recipes.htm.

- **If you usually drive or go somewhere (like the pub) to drink, then it should be easy to just change that habit altogether**. Go to the gym or to the park after work. Take your dog for a walk. Or begin a hobby to look forward to getting to after work.

- **Do you usually drink more around certain people?** Determine why you tend to drink more around these people (for instance, they make you anxious) and plan what you can do to deal with their personalities. Or perhaps they drink a lot and it makes you want to drink also. Alternate nonalcoholic beverages or recommend activities you can do with these people besides drink. If you have to, reduce the amount of time you spend with them.

These are just a few ideas to get you started. The main idea is to do things you enjoy; don't turn this into yet another painful task or problem to solve, or it will backfire. Look at this instead as an opportunity to live life completely alert and aware of the pleasures that it can hold!

GET OUT OF THE RUT AND DUMP THE BAGGAGE

TAKE-AWAY CHECKLIST
1. Use pain as a motivation for change, not for drinking.
2. Determine what you are trying to avoid.
3. Make a plan for how to change the situation.
4. Take action.

One thing we have to be aware of is that pain and negative emotions serve a purpose—to signal a bad or uncomfortable situation—and make us aware something needs to change. Drinking to deal with the pain only serves to keep us paralyzed or even makes things worse. Not only do relations and relationships get strained due to your drinking, but also your thought process is impaired. Even long after a drinking binge, although we may be sober, the residual effects from the alcohol tend to make us more paranoid and lack the ability to see things objectively.

Here are a few steps for dealing with the issues from which you're trying to escape:

Step 1: Determine what it is you're trying to avoid by drinking.
For example:
- Devastation about a life-threatening disease, either yours or a loved-one's.

- Major conflicting views with spouse on a critical issue, such as raising the children.

- Negative or unfulfilling work situation (pay, boss, type of work).

- Unresolved emotional baggage. Sometimes it's easier to focus or obsess on an addiction than deal with the underlying baggage, such as physical or sexual abuse from childhood, or the early death of a loved one.

- Your own inner voice—negative self-talk. For whatever reason, we're overly critical of ourselves, feeling that we have to be perfect—thin enough, smart enough, successful enough.

- Abuse.

Step 2: Decide what it will take to get out of the situation or change it. For example:
- **Devastation about a life-threatening disease**. It may help to see a therapist for a session or two, or join a support group.

- **Major conflicting views with spouse on a critical issue.** Don't stop working on it; keep communicating and come to an acceptable compromise, if necessary.

- **Negative or unfulfilling work situation.** Begin researching other employers or careers. I personally like the book *Your Dream Career for Dummies* by Carol L. McClelland, Ph.D.[10]

- **Emotional baggage**. It will probably require a therapist to help you dig this up and begin healing.

- **Your own inner voice.** Begin adopting a feeling of self-love and tolerance. Realize what is "good enough."

- **Abuse**. Abuse, whether physical or emotional, is *never acceptable or justifiable*. Drinking to tolerate abuse only makes the situation worse and makes you feel worse about yourself.
  - Physical Abuse: Get help and get safe!
  - Emotional/Verbal Abuse: Get help!
    - It can be as simple as training someone how to treat you. There are many self-help books. I like *The Commitment Chronicles* by Cheryl McClary, Ph.D.[11]
    - However, some abusers can't be taught. Do what you have to do to take care of yourself, including getting out of the relationship. Discuss your situation with a therapist or support group.

Step 3: Start taking steps to make the changes. Remember that the shortest way around something is through it. Don't drink to self-medicate. It will not fix the problem; it will only make it worse. If you're feeling stressed or anxious, take MODER8, go for a walk, or do any number of the things you may have discovered in "Strategy IV: Things to Do Instead of Drink."

Whatever you do, **don't waste anymore of your life by drowning your emotions. Put the bottle down and start taking action.**

STRATEGY VII:

SUPPORT AND GETTING OUT OF ISOLATION

SEEK SUPPORT

Seek support for the new changes and lifestyle that you are trying to implement. It is best to seek encouragement from someone or some group that will be supportive of your goals and strategy—someone that understands what you are going through and has had some of the same experiences.

See if there are any local Moderation Management (MM) meetings in your area, or join an online forum. The MODER8 website (MODER8NOW. COM) offers an online support community for clients that have purchased the three- or six-month starter kits or are repeat customers. The reason for this requirement for membership is to weed out the people that are just looking for another quick fix and gather those who are willing to make some changes and do a little work.

Other free online support forums that are available for people that are trying to drink in moderation are HAMSNETWORK.ORG and MYWAYOUT. ORG.

BREAKING FREE OF THE SHAME AND THE SPIRAL OF OUT-OF-CONTROL DRINKING

Is shame keeping you stuck in the self-destructive habit of drinking uncontrollably? Perhaps you've done some things that were embarrassing, hurtful, or dangerous in the past because of alcohol. You may have even been given the label "alcoholic" and told that you can't control your drinking. Labels do nothing more than create a negative sense of who you are and shame you. And where there is shame, there is a need to self-medicate and try to escape from ourselves.

You have to begin to change the way you see and think about yourself and drinking (See "Strategy I: Change the Way You Think about Alcoholism"). It is important for two main reasons:

1) What you think affects your actions. (For more on this topic, visit Mike Dooley's "Thoughts Become Things," http://www. thoughtsbecomethings.com).[12]

2) Shame and feeling negatively about yourself causes more pain and eventually leads to more drinking to escape the painful feelings (visit www.bestyears.com/shame/html for more on "shame.")

So where do you start to break this cycle?

1) Know that you are not a label. Drinking alcohol is a behavior—it is not who you are.

2) Realize who you are and what you want to be.

3) Apologize to those that you may have hurt in the past and commit to yourself to start making changes.

4) Make the changes to correct the bad habits or behaviors.

5) Stop the self-judgment. Replace negative thoughts about yourself with positive thoughts. Practice using positive affirmations. Tell yourself that you are smart, attractive, loveable, kind, worthy, or whatever you need to hear.

6) Learn from your mistakes and continue to do the things that work (for example, take MODER8, plan your drinking and personal goals, and find things to do for fun or relaxation besides drink)

7) Realize that today is a new day and a new opportunity to be the person you want to be. Control your drinking instead of allowing your drinking to control you.

GET RID OF THE SECRETS AND BREAK OUT OF ISOLATION
There's a common saying I've heard around twelve-step meetings: "In our secrets lies our disease." I personally feel that the term *disease* comes loaded with way too many alternate meanings attached, many implying that we are helpless and have no control over our situation. I prefer to say, "In our secrets lies our self-imposed prison."

How many of you have bottles of wine or liquor hidden in your house or other private places? "Renee" used to keep bottles of red wine hidden in her laundry room cabinets, stashed behind the bleach and the extra supply of paper towels. (It's amazing how much more "pleasant" folding clothes can be while sipping on a nice Cabernet! Of course, now that she has control of her drinking and no longer needs to sneak it, her laundry seems to be piling up). Or how many of you have learned how to dispose of your empty bottles so that they won't "clink" in the trash bag, or how to hide the alcohol on your breath with menthol cough drops because the medicinal smell of ethanol is too strong to be hidden by chewing gum? I've heard these stories and more from many who could master in the art of espionage!

So why do we feel so compelled to hide our drinking problem? Perhaps you know that your professional credibility would be shot if someone knew. Or it may be that the other parents in the neighborhood or school would never trust you with their child. We all have valid reasons, but they will keep us locked away in our dungeon until we get rid of this bondage.

Isolation is one of our greatest enemies. It allows negative and paranoid thoughts to run rampant through our minds and destroys us from the inside out like a plague.

WHERE TO START:
Step 1—Find someone *safe* with whom you can share your secret...*not* someone that will feel compelled to fix you or dish out "shame" or "condemnation" or that throw it back in your face next time you have a disagreement.

Some examples:

- Your doctor. If you're concerned about it showing up in your medical record, ask your doctor not to record it in your file. Doctors see addiction problems all the time, and they usually don't judge you or your character. They may have some good advice.

- Someone that you trust that you know has dealt with addiction.

- Your counselor or therapist.

- An Internet community where you can remain anonymous, such as the MODER8 Support Community, HAMSNETWORK.ORG, or MYWAYOUT.ORG.

- A priest or pastor (this can be a little bit tricky, depending on your religion, the size of your church, etc. Listen to your gut first).

Step 2—Forgive yourself. There's nothing wrong with you because you have a drinking problem! The faster you can realize that and move on, the more successful you'll be in gaining control over your drinking.

Step 3—Know that you can overcome. Trust me, if I can, I know that you can!

Step 4—Start working on a plan.
- Begin working through some of the exercises in this book.

- Start taking MODER8 or other dietary supplements.

- Follow some suggestions that may seem helpful to you in some of the blog articles on the MODER8NOW.com and other websites.

- Go to your favorite online bookstore and search for material to address your issues.

You may be surprised what letting go of these skeletons will do for you. But if you don't at least take the first step, you won't know what an incredible freedom there is out there waiting for you!

TOOLS TO *KEEP* YOUR DRINKING UNDER CONTROL

STAY POSITIVE

It's so important that you stay positive and focus on your progress and successes, no matter how small they may be. If you used to drink ten beers a day and now you're only drinking six, that is progress! And focusing on your progress builds your confidence and helps you continue to improve.

Try not to have too high of expectations or you could be setting yourself up for shame and all-or-nothing behavior. Instead, continue focusing on your goals and visions and taking the steps to make those happen.

There is no "perfect" way to drink in moderation or control your drinking!

BACKSLIDES

- **Don't panic**. Backslides happen to just about everyone. The most important thing to remember is *NOT TO PANIC!* Panic causes us to become ineffective because we don't think straight and it launches self-destructive actions and behavior.

- **Learn from it**. Focus on what works and what doesn't. Instead of dwelling on the negative, learn from it!

- **Get rid of the whip and stop beating yourself up.** Today is a new day; yesterday is gone. You have the opportunity to start completely over and do it the way you had planned today! (See **Motivation Resuscitation**.) But most importantly, do not beat yourself up! Self-judgment only results in shame and feeling helpless, worthless, and out of control. If you don't want to be around yourself, guess what you're going to do to get away from you—probably drink.

PRACTICE, PRACTICE, PRACTICE—STAY IN TUNE WITH YOURSELF AND REMAIN VIGILANT

Maintain self-awareness. Know what's going on with you and where your urges are coming from. If you're saying to yourself, "I just really want a drink," then learn how to figure out what's causing that urge. It is often an emotion that could be dealt with in a healthy manner, or it could be as simple as the fact that you're hungry, thirsty, or bored.

Just keep practicing, staying self-aware, and using the outlined strategies and behavior changes instead of turning to alcohol to medicate. Make it your mission to become the person you want to be without depending on alcohol, and eventually you'll have complete and total control over drinking. Your life will be balanced and content.

TAKE CARE OF YOU AND YOUR HEALTH

Incorporate a healthy diet and some moderate exercise into your life. Begin taking care of yourself instead of punishing yourself for drinking. The nicer you treat yourself, the better you'll feel about yourself instead of drinking to escape your own self-judgment and mistreatment. It's really about self-love.

APPENDIX:

ESPECIALLY FOR MOMS—FINDING THE

RIGHT BALANCE AND TAKING CARE OF YOU!

What is it about moms that make us think that in order for us to be good enough, we have to make sure that everyone else is happy, while neglecting ourselves? Neglecting ourselves includes medicating with alcohol because our inner voices are screaming for a break, but we won't give it to them.

Maybe it comes from wanting it all. Or maybe it comes from low self-worth because of our shame from being dependent on alcohol. Maybe it's because a huge part of society tells us our place is at home with the family, but yet we still want and need something that is our own. (I had a friend whose husband had a religious exorcism performed on her to get rid of the "demon" that was causing her to want to work!) There is always more laundry to fold, more dishes to wash, and more groceries to buy. Where is the sense of accomplishment in that? I'm not sure, but as the number of soccer-mom DUIs increases, I become more aware that this generation of moms needs to make some changes.

Many of us were driven as young women to excel in school or a sport. For many of us, our identity was dependent on our level of performance. Then we went to college or specialty school and developed our education or craft even further. We dreamt of how successful we would be. Then we graduated from school or college and began to move into our careers or areas of interest. We began climbing the career ladder, succeeding in our fields or specialties, and then Mother Nature said "Hey! You're getting older! Don't you think you should get married?" So some of us married our high school or college sweethearts, some of us married someone because the time was right and we just didn't want to date anymore, and some of us married because we really thought we were in love and it was the thing to do. Even though we were married, we still maintained our own identity for the most part, and then Mother Nature called again: "Hey, if you're going to have children, you'd better do it now!" So we had children and a whole new meaning to the word "love" emerged! Then the internal tug-of-war began. Somehow you, your wants, dreams, needs, and desires got lost.

How do you become all things to all the people in your life? Your husband, your boss, your children, your customers—they all have demands and expectations of you. But do you know the demands and expectations that are the most difficult to deal with? The demands and expectations that *you* put on *yourself*!

It's time to lighten up! Give yourself a break and give yourself permission to enjoy life (and I mean *really* experience it—not just go through the motions in some kind of alcohol-induced coma)!

The answer to your stress is not in the bottle! Fight for your right to live a happy, balanced life, and be in control of alcohol.

Begin to get back in touch with your needs, wants, and dreams. Here's a good place to start:

1) **Get off your case**. Stop trying to be Super Mom and be nice to yourself instead.

2) **Stop the negative self talk.** Would you call someone you love "fat, old, stupid, ugly, etc."? Of course not, so don't call yourself those things.

3) **Learn how to say "No."** There will always be someone else that can do that volunteer position. If you are doing it because you need to get out of isolation and to feel productive, then go for it. But if you're doing it so someone will like you or so you won't feel guilty, then forget it. You are the only one that can and will take care of you and your commitment to control your drinking.

4) **Re-energize yourself**. I've also heard it called "refilling your love bucket." Do peaceful, loving things for yourself in order to have the love that you give out to everyone else everyday.

5) **Start identifying the fun things you like to do**. I recently discovered that I like to read teen fantasy romance novels; I'm not sure what it says about my emotional maturity, but I don't really care—it's fun to me.)

6) **Schedule some time in your day to then do those things that you think are fun.**

7) **Nurture or pamper yourself**. Get a spa pedicure or massage. If money is an issue, ask your children or your husband to brush your hair or give you a hand massage.

8) **Form a Mom's Group**. Women need to talk about their lives and their feelings (men do too, they just don't usually admit it). Schedule a regular coffee or lunch session with some of your friends. I joined a book club that meets monthly to have lunch and "discuss the book we've read." We're considering changing the name to our "lunch club with recommended reading," because we rarely spend more than five minutes discussing our book. Most of the two to three hours is spent talking about our families and parenting issues. It's very therapeutic and we always feel re-energized when we leave the meeting.

9) **Get Motivated.** Have you lost sight of your dreams and passions? Go to the "Rekindling Your Dreams" section of "Strategy III: Getting Motivated."

These are just a few ideas. I know you've heard them before, but you have to actually *do* them! I am in no way telling you to neglect your other relationships or responsibilities; I simply know that you have to take care of you *first*!

NOTES AND REFERENCES

1. Miller, Scott D. and Insoo Kim Berg. *The Miracle Method: A Radically New Approach to Problem Drinking*, 16. New York: W. W. Norton & Company, 1995.

2. MacDonald, Lilian, and Murdock MacDonald. Cambridgeshire, UK. *Phoenix in a Bottle*. Melrose Books, 2009.

3. Peele, Stanton Peele. *The Stanton Peele Addiction Website*. Accessed October 2010.

4. Miller and Berg. *The Miracle Method*, 27.

5. Blum, Kenneth, et al. *Nutritional Gene Therapy: Natural Healing in Recovery*. www.counselormagazine.com, 2001.

6. Goldstein, Avram. *Addiction: from Biology to Drug Policy*, 66–69. New York: Oxford University Press, 2001.

7. Amen, Daniel. *Change Your Brain, Change Your Body*, 50. New York: Harmony Books, 2010.

8. Davich, Victor N. *The Best Guide to Meditation*. New York: St. Martin's Griffin, 1998.

9. Peeke, Pamela. *Body for Life for Women*, 68. New York: Rodale, 2005.

10. McClessand, Carol L. *Your Dream Career for Dummies*. Indianapolis, IN: Wiley Publishing, Inc., 2005.

11. McClary, Cheryl. *The Commitment Chronicles: The Power of Staying Together*. Naperville, IL: Sourcebooks, Inc., 2006.

12. Dooley, Mike. *Thoughts Become Things* (DVD). Orlando: TUT Enterprises, Inc., 2009.

RECOMMENDED READING
The Miracle Method: A Radically New Approach to Problem Drinking, Scott D. Miller and Insoo Kim Berg

Change Your Brain, Change Your Body, Daniel G. Amen

Body for Life for Women, Pamela Peeke

How to Change Your Drinking: A Harm Reduction Guide to Alcohol, Kenneth Anderson

The Best Guide to Meditation, Victor N. Davich

RECOMMENDED WEBSITES
www.MODER8NOW.com

http://peele.net/about/index.html

http://hamsnetwork.org

http://rethinkingdrinking.niaaa.nih.gov/IsYourDrinkingPatternRisky/WhatsLowRiskDrinking.asp

www.bestyears.com/shame/html

ABOUT THE AUTHOR

Elizabeth Michael is the President of Second Chance Health and Wellness, Inc.

With degrees in biochemistry and biology, she has extensive experience as an analytical chemist and formulator. While this professional expertise has aided in the development of MODER8, it is Elizabeth's personal experience with alcohol that has been the driving force behind its creation.

Like an estimated twenty million Americans, Elizabeth Michael abused alcohol. As with many substance abusers, Elizabeth's struggles with alcohol began at an early age, resulting in academic suspensions and legal problems. Parental intervention and professional counseling had little effect on her desire for alcohol. Finally, at the age of twenty-one, Elizabeth joined Alcoholics Anonymous. Two years of sobriety followed, but eventually she returned to drinking.

Then a miracle occurred. Elizabeth began researching neurotransmitters in the brain and their role in controlling addictions, including alcoholism. Using her background in biochemistry, her findings allowed her to develop the proprietary blend in MODER8.

The results were astonishing. For the first time in her life, Elizabeth was able to drink only one glass of wine and be completely satisfied. Since she began taking MODER8, the most alcohol she has consumed in one day is three drinks, and she now goes many days without drinking any alcohol at all.

Today, Elizabeth is determined to share MODER8, as well as the skills and strategies that she has identified, to help people regain control of their lives—just as she has.

I N D E X

CPSIA information can be obtained
at www.ICGtesting.com
Printed in the USA
FSOW04n0847270416
19750FS

9 781456 375416